L'ACADEMIE OF ¡IMAGINACIÓN!

DAVID CHEN

南郭求敗

An Academy of Imagination
想象力研究院

ISBN: 978-0-9861612-7-8

Copyright: Empty Air Clean Energy (EacE) LLC, 2020

空气能源净化环保(统易龙)公司·版权所有·2020

Claim the Earth series

《玩世》系列丛书

I am I

You are you

He is he

我是我，你是你，他是他

Objects at rest tend to stay at rest

Objects in motion tend to stay in motion

静者趋静 动者趋动

In a confined system, energy stays constant

封闭系统中，能量不可能凭空产生或消失

CONTENTS

ACKNOWLEDGMENTS i

1 IMAGINATION 1

2 ABSTRACT ALGEBRA FOR BEGINNERS 4

    对称 4

    维 5

    空 6

    内外 7

    对偶 7

3 UNIVERSE(S) 10

4 LIFE 14

5 GRAND UNIFIED THEORY 16

6 PERPETUAL-PHOBIA 20

7 301 CONJECTURE 22

8 SCIENCE OF DIVIDING BY 0 – study of dimensions 25

9 SYMMETRY AND ASYMMETRY 30

10 VIRTUAL WORK AND REAL WORK 32

11 A NEW INDUSTRY 34

12 RELIGION, SCIENCE & IMAGINATION 43

13 TRUE AND FALSE 46

14 UNITY AND FUTURE 48

ABOUT THE AUTHOR 53

Que sera sera

Whatever will be will be

人法地 地法天 天法道 道法自然

There's no acceleration without outside force

学如逆水行舟 不进则退

Heat does not flow from low temperature to high temperature

In a confined system, entropy cannot decrease

人往高处走 水往低处流

ACKNOWLEDGMENTS

This book would not have been possible without the entire humanity happen to exist in the same space-time in such a proximity to the authors. Closer to the concepts that we call "here" and "now", larger amounts of gratitude are expressed from the authors.

Force of action equals to force of reaction.

作用力等于反作用力。

In the universe, absolute 0 in kelvin scale is not achievable, nor is absolute vacuum.

宇宙中，开氏温度的绝对 0 度是不可能达到的，绝对真空也是不存在的。

Nothing ever exists alone, not even God, therefore these is never such thing as singularity

天尊地卑 乾坤定矣。

1 IMAGINATION
(想象力)

Imagination rules the world is a translation from the phrase "L'imagination gouverne le monde" or "L'imaginaire gouverne le monde".

Other profound and popular phrases about imagination include: "seeing is believing" or "a picture is worth a thousand words", etc.

In Chinese, the words for imagination can be literally translated as "the ability to think about an entire elephant", which leads to the story of several blind men and an elephant:

The moral of the story is: if you can look at truth from different perspective, your vision of truth is closer to what it really is. Therefore, the importance of learning multiple languages is: if you can understand different languages in the world, you would have a better chance of understanding what the language of God is truly trying to convey.

中国古代称"象"为"南越大兽"。"想象力"是一种在脑海中绘制、构思一幅巨大图像的力量。

Galileo Galilei once expressed that "mathematics is the language of God", which lead us to believe that language can be always drawn in pictures, a.k.a. "images". To understand or to think is to possess imagination. To learn science is to learn to possess imagination, and once imagination is achieved, many, many universes can be created out of them.

學好數理化
走遍天下都不怕

学好数理化
走遍天下都不怕

学好数理化
走遍天下都不怕

Chinese language has many "perspectives" or "dimensions". The look of it is "imagination", the sound of it is "phonetics". Correspondingly, there are "reading" and "writing", which offer one perspective of imagination, and "listening" and "speaking", which offer yet another perspective.

锥棍柱扇刷鞭毯　子子子子子子子

Out of the Chinese encoding/decoding system, there is also the "dimension" or "perspective" of tonal changes. Each contemporary Chinese "word" consists of one syllable and it can have one of the following tones.

中文声调:

1   2   3   4

Once you have grasped the meaning of the above chart, try to read out loud the following words, and match them with the picturesque descriptions of the above elephant.

zhui(1)zhi(0)
gun(4)zhi(0)
zhu(4)zhi(0)
shan(4)zhi(0)
shua(1)zhi(0)
bian(1)zhi(0)
tan(3)zhi(0)

The above pronunciations match the order of the Chinese characters but does not match the order of the numbers in the picture. It can be used as an exercise to connect images with sounds for beginners learning Chinese in an entry class.

2 ABSTRACT ALGEBRA FOR BEGINNERS
（抽象代数入门）

When the unknowns in some simple algebraic equation are solved, the solutions are usually numbers. When the unknowns in abstract algebraic problems are solved, the solutions could be "sets", "groups", "matrix", "people", "teams", "society", "polity", countries", "climate" or even "universe"

所谓"抽象代数"，是指计算或"算计"一些抽象的数，集合，结构，物质，生物，个体/单体 – 到集体，人物，事件，社会。。。等等等等的学问。

不管在二十世纪被人们称为"万事万物理论"（theory of everything）也好，还是被叫做"群众理论"（group theory）也好，最终到了二十一世纪人们发觉，这些"计算"和"算计"都不会像简单的一维 的思维中，数字的简单加减乘除一样有一个准确的"决定论"的答案。多维的矩阵、集合 或数据结构运算的结果往往是反"决定论"的，相对的、量子的、不连续的、测不准的一些答案。计算结果不是静止的，而是随时变化着的。没有真相，只有概率，没有绝对的准确，只有相对的可信度。想通了这一点，就会发觉抽象代数的矩阵运算的结果与现实生活中观察到的实验现象惊人的接近和吻合。当然还是要再重申一下，这种"吻合"不会是 100% 的精确，仍然是"测不准定律"控制下的很高的概率和置信度而已。接受和承认"测不准"的遗憾和欠缺，是人类思维从原子时代进入量子时代的一大飞跃。

对称

除了人们常常想到的和常常说到的"镜像"对称以外，日常生活中常常遇到的"对称"还包括：旋转对称、成比例对称 – 和最重要的"自对称"。

algebra, especially "abstract algebra" is the study of symmetry.

在阿拉伯语中，الجبر 音 al-jabr，有"还原、修复"的意思。好像精心制作的零件经过翻转、打磨、放大缩小最后能够吻合上一个适合的位置。中文中的"代数"有着"代替"与原有的扮演的角色"相符合"也指的是类似的意思。

古希腊人们所提到的"对称"，细细分析起来是由"sym"和"metry"两部分组成的。前一部分听起来像"same""similar"后一部分听起来像"metrics""measure"。所以，欧洲人心中的"对称"就是："相同尺寸"，"测量结果符合"的意思。

Beauty is truth, truth beauty.

据说这就是希腊人说的对称。

维

提起"维"，很容易让人想到的是笛卡尔坐标系中的 X Y Z，三根坐标轴。在 20 世纪爱因斯坦提出了相对论之后，越来越多的人们会想到宇宙是一个 XYZ-t 四维的坐标系。平心静气地想一想，抽象地归纳一下，"维"究竟是个什么东西呢？

抽象地说，用老中的观点，"维"就是一个可以类比的"群"、"集合"。说：一头猪，一匹马，一头牛...就给宇宙定义了三个"维"。每一个量词，就定义着一个"维"。

A dimension is a vector space, or simply put it, a reference frame set. It can also be called a group, a set, a matrix . . . and a category of many other things.

在爱因斯坦以前，拉普拉斯以及传统的"决定论"者的心中，XYZ-t 这样的线性代数坐标系中，维与维之间必须"线性无关，垂直相交"。爱因斯坦是一个桥梁似的人物，提出了相对论，但是仍然坚持决定论的："宇宙连续"的观点；引发了量子力学的研究，又压制了"宇宙不连续"的矩阵、行列式的宇宙观和宇宙坐标系。爱老的名言之一包括："God does not roll dice"，就是针对量子理论的。

正像"地球围着太阳转"这样革命性的观点提出来以后，人类越看越觉得像有这么回事一样，"宇宙是不连续的"观点对于西方的教庭、西方文化也是一个革命性的观点。在新的一个对偶的向量的时空中，人类又一次越看越觉得像有那么会事。

A dimension in the universe does not have to be continuous, and that is the "quantum leap" of human knowledge in the 21st century.

既然宇宙的"坐标系/参照系"中的"坐标点/参照物"不是连续的，那么维与维之间的"线性无关、垂直相交"的条件就不是很难满足了。维与维之间，不"垂直相交"的时候，也可以"线性无关"，因为宇宙是不连续的，其中充满了空洞，无论谁的变化，与别的人和事的变化，长远看来都是"线性无关"的。想通了这一点以后，我们就会发现，以抽象代数的观点看，宇宙中岂止是只有 XYZ-t 那么四维？群与群之间，集合与集合之间，类与类之间，矩阵与矩阵之间都是线性无关的。向外看，宇宙中简直有着数不清的的无数多"维"。向内看，一根坐标轴上 $\{x|x<0\}$ 和 $\{x|x>0\}$ 两个对偶的向量空间，也是线性无关的，也形成了两"维"。

God does not play dice. I bet he loves flipping coins. 阴阳，长短，有无，前后，虚实，过去、将来…

空

"维"与"维"之间是通过"空"连接起来的。比如，ＸＹＺ坐标轴，通过一个"0"点相交。抽象地看这种"空"和"维"的关系，其实可以给我们很大的启示。

在 20 世纪前，人类普遍以为宇宙不是相对的，时间就更是绝对的。爱因斯坦提出相对论以后，人们开始怀疑宇宙的绝对性。但是后来量子的理论依然受到人们普遍的怀疑，说明绝大多数人仍然不能相信宇宙中，尤其是时间这一维，也就是历史中，充满了不连续、间断、空洞、干扰、偶然性、和测不准。

21 世纪后，随着量子理论的发展，随着人们对"维"和"空"之间的关系有了更多的理解，就很容易发现宇宙中到处都是"空"了。在已知 x=5 的情况下，将本来在 x=0 处的 Y 坐标轴，平移到 x=5 的位置，做为新的 Y 坐标轴。最后在相对的思维中，脑海中浮现的图像就是：X 和 Y 坐标轴的交接，就在原来等于 5 的那个点上。这么一来，5 就成了"空"。所以用相对的量子的观点来看，人们可以说万事皆空。还有万物之中也充满了空。正好像正数和负数之间的交接部位就是零。那么上下、前后、左右、长短、高低、大小……等等等等，各"维"可思想的矩阵相量空间中，很容易找到和产生相对的真空的现象。

而"阴阳不测之谓神"，"悟空神通广大"，以前人类思维中所不能理解的一些生命现象和社会现象，在 21 世纪后都有了更合理的解释。而新理论的应用也会给人类的生活带来更高的文明和更多的幸福。

内外

"In" and "out" often give one observer two opposite images of truth at the same time.

据道听途说得来的梵文知识中记载：把嘴张大到不能再大了，发一个音，然后再把嘴闭到不能再闭了，又发一个音。两个音连起来发，就形成了今天世上存活的几大宗教，祈祷时像神发出的心声：om 阿弥 阿门 阿明

哥白尼，伽利略，牛顿 都讨论过一个在航行的大船上向上抛的球，又沿着直线直直地落下的现象。而在岸上的观察者眼中，这个球是沿着一条抛物线起落的。这是"航海时代"开始给人们带来的，内外不同的两幅观察现象。船内的人观察到、感觉到的是静止；船外的人观察到、感觉到的是运动。

航海时代继续向前进，达尔文看到了遗传和变异，这是生命现象中的内和外。"自己"要坚持是"自己"，也就是人们常说的"自保"，保持"自我存在" – 向内部看就是生物的不变、保守、遗传。向外看就是一代一代之间的分娩、新生，以及随之产生的变异。

从无机世界到有机世界，自对称是动力，内外所观察到的是千变万化五彩缤纷的别的形式的对称。"自己是自己"：静者，趋静；动者，趋动。这说的就是牛顿第一定律，也叫惯性定律。再想一想，我是我，你是你，他是他。其实也是能量守恒定律，也叫热力学第一定律。还有"该怎样就怎样"，这种充满智慧的说法，其实也就是热力学第二定律。

抽象地说，"内"和"外"，"封闭体系"和"开放体系"，是一个很重要的一个"维"中的两个对偶的向量空间。所谓"一生二，二生三，三生万物"，"内外"的思维使"二生三"的飞跃成为可能。在内外两个不同的参照系中看，真相和假象，竟然可以重合叠加，使人达到新的认知高度，获得更多的智慧，感知新的存在，产生新的生命。正所谓：

横看成岭侧成峰 远近高低各不同

不识庐山真面目 只缘生在此山中

对偶

Dual vector space/time

有了内外的概念之后，所有存在的物体，都不难想象有着外部的环境。以数学这样的上帝的语言来描述，每一个数周围都有着许多别的数排列成的矩阵或行列式。二十世纪与过去相比，人类思想上最大的飞跃就是意识到了：所谓时间，也是一种矩阵排列成的向量空间。对偶的向量（或矢量）空间 - dual vector space/time – 就是指两个不同的，但组成结构类似的矩阵空间，其中同样的运算法则可以适用。保罗·狄拉克以 $<\varphi|\psi>$ 这样的符号来表示。任何物体都同时处在"运动"和"静止"两种状态之中。缺少了两种状态中的任何一种状态的描述，都不是对整个量子状态的一种完整的描述。

对偶的概念掌握了以后，便很容易理解"一生二 二生三 三生万物"的道理是怎么来的。还有关于"对称"是一种对偶的特例，也很容易理解了。

量子理论的 duality 的描述提出来之后，如同地球围着太阳转的现象被哥白尼指出来以后一样，觉得在日常生活中司空见惯，习以为常，越来越多的人恍然大悟，然后逻辑思维，以及生活方式上都发生了革命性的彻底的变化。"一阴一阳之谓道，阴阳不测之谓神"。阴阳一体，就像一个硬币的两面，是同时存在、相生相克、不断转换却有离不开的。举一些例子：

坐地日行八万里。当每个人在银河系中，觉得我们处在静止状态的时候，其实我们是在飞速地运动着的。

春夏秋冬，南北半球观察到的结果是对偶的。当一个人在某地经历一个季节时，到了另一个南北半球，所经历的就会是一个对偶的季节。

白天黑夜，东西半球，当一个半球处在白天的时候，另一个半球就处在黑夜里。

人往高处走，难道我们身边每个人真的都这样吗？

水往低处流，身边的花草树木，生命现象里的水，是否也总往低处流？云兴霞蔚，雾气蒸腾，又是怎么回事？百川归海说的是海，黄山云海说的也是海。泰山顶上一青松是在歌颂生命力，为什么黄山扑面迎客松，能使人感到黄山归来不看岳？反者道之动，有点像原子能的释放；弱者道之用，似乎有点像在描述量子能源。

当我们以为我们找到了真相的时候，其实跳出我们所处的环境观察，很可能就发现我们生活在假象之中。

"真"和"假"其实竟然是同一回事，同为一体，那么别的"怪现象"还有什么好说的、好想的、难理解的呢？

回到<"数学是上帝的语言" | "语文是老天爷加码、解码的信息通讯法则"> 这种对抽象代数的理解和讨论中：在对偶的向量空间里的计算，其实很像中国学者们在文学中常玩的那种游戏"对对子"，也就是在不同的环境、意境、矩阵空间中，做对偶的"计算"和"算计"。

海阔凭鱼跃

天高任鸟飞

<海 | 天>是对偶的的矩阵向量空间。鱼和鸟是代进去计算的对偶的数。跃和飞，则是对偶的运算法则。

不同的人造对偶的句子，根据自己的生活经历，思想境界的不同，也就是坐标系和参照系的不同，会对出不同的结果。

心比天高

身为下贱

是一种对对子的说法，也有另外的多种对偶的说法可以说成是：

心比天高；志入云霄；行如海阔……

3 UNIVERSE(S)
(宇宙观)

Theory of everything

Theory: **观点**

Everything: **宇宙**

Somebody once said: "boundary of language is the boundary of my world". And somebody else said, "math is the alphabet of the language God used to describe the universe ".

With the existence of the above statements, while living in the 21st-century, it is easy to imagine the universe as an encoding and decoding system with numbers being used to carry information and conduct communications. What do we call such a system? "A giant computer!", some blind man would imagine, "a giant matrix!" some others would utter...

语言上说，中国人所说的宇宙，上下四方称为"宇"，古往今来谓之"宙"。所以在中文中的"宇宙"是"空间"和"时间"的集合，是地地道道的"spacetime"，这个 20 世纪西方现代科学中提出来的相对论的观点。

Linguistically, "universe" in English means "uni" and "verse", "same and opposite at the same time". Understanding this word has puzzled me for quite a long time, as to why "quantum mechanics" was so vehemently rejected by Western scientific community for such a long time. Being "true and false at the same time" or being "dead and alive at the same time" is such a simple concept. How come there are so many people having such a difficult time understanding it? Like any body-part of an elephant, its shape and form can be portrayed as "true and false at the same time", depending on whether the observer is looking at it, from near or from afar, from inside or from outside. When the great Albert Einstein described the universe as "everything is relative", he was also describing "everything is quantized" at the same time. The "Grand Unified Theory", which brings theory of relativity and quantum mechanics together, should have been proposed right there and then. Mr Einstein did bring to the world theory of "relativity and quantum" together in 1905 as "theory of light":

$$mc^2 = E = h\nu$$

Ironically, it was also for a major part because of Mr. Einstein's objections and his reputation, the Grand Unified Theory" which defines the universe as being both "relative and quantized at the same time" had to wait for more than another 100 years to be brought to the world.

无论是以东方的"时空"这样的概念来定义宇宙还是把宇宙理解为是"对立统一"（universe)这样的西方传统概念，宇宙都是一个对偶的概念(duality)，不可能产生于一个所谓的"singularity"。认为宇宙中曾经有过一次大爆炸，在负责任的科学家心中是不可想象的。大爆炸理论最有说服力的证据-红移现象-只不过是 Roger Bacon 提出过的 "every point on earth is the center of its own horizon"，的 2 维现象在 3 维空间中的显影。

更合理的一个宇宙模型，在测不准原理和广义相对论效果叠加了以后应该是：宇宙是一个大范围内布朗运动造成的大漩涡，有着许多局部的可能的不小的爆炸。

在不受外力影响的情况下，漩涡周围的物质，最后总会漩向中心。但是那将会是在很长、很长时间以后。

地球周围也许曾经有过不止一个月亮，最后都会被漩到地球中去，但是那将会是在很长、很长时间以后。

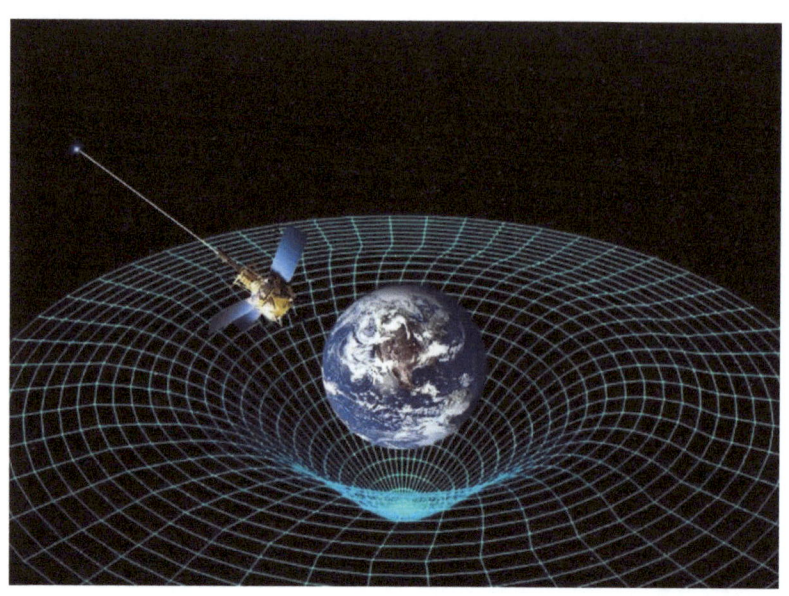

地球和其他的行星，最终都将被漩到太阳中去，但是那将会是在更长、更长时间以后。

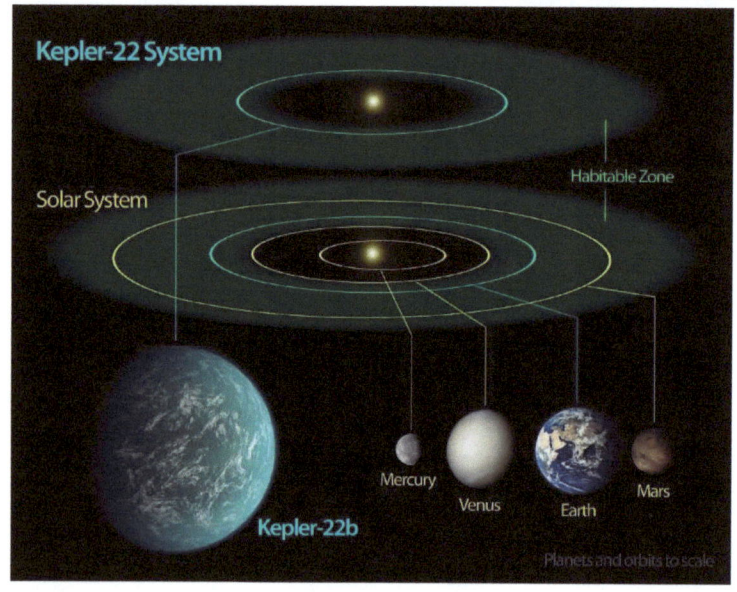

绝对的平行宇宙是不存在的，因为最终他们都将会被漩到一处。相对的平行宇宙却有许多，就

是那些还没被漩到一块儿的大大小小的天体或宇宙尘埃。

漩涡的中心是黑洞。黑洞密度很大，但是质量可大可小，因为黑洞的体积可大可小，是测不准的。黑洞也会发光，也就是黑体辐射。辐射出来的能量多少，速度多快也是测不准的。如果黑洞的质量足够大，有可能再引起一次局部的爆炸。如果黑洞的质量不够大，有可能就被渐渐地磨损掉了。黑洞的结局也是测不准的。

如果局部的爆炸发生了，那么又可以有很长很长的一段时期，形成一些巨大巨大的漩涡，围着漩涡的中心旋转。这样的过程周而复始，永无止境。所以绝对时空是不存在的。宇宙在时间和空间上，没有起点也没有终点。

4 LIFE
（生命观）

Certain structures and events they go through

一定的结构 + 新陈代谢

Those are the opinions expressed by Erwin Schrodinger in his famous short pamphlet "what is life?".

Another more advanced view about life is that it is permeating in the universe as animated "animals". The ancient sage who thought life was everywhere happened to get his own life burned out of him, and his name is Giordano Bruno.

无机和有机的物质当然都有生命，或者说寿命吧。说有机物有生命，大家习以为常。说到无机物有生命，提醒一下，大家也就觉得很有道理了。比如我们会说某种元素的半衰期，就是有一半的某种同位素元素，生命结束的时间长短。既然元素都有生命，那就所有的无机物都有生命了。

所有的生命形式都希望"维持"和"维生"，也就是保持"自己是自己"。想要"自己是自己"大致有着两条路：

1）不变；

2）变化，但是周而复始地循环往复地变回自己。

以上所说的，第 2）种变化形式是我们所熟悉的生命形式，也就是有机物的生命形式，比如：DNA、微生物、植物、哺乳动物。第 1）种"不变化"的生命形式，其实也存在着变化。因为宇宙中是不可能存在不变化的物体的。只是无机物有可能变化周期太长，变化频率太慢，无法被察觉而已。这一种以"不变"的方法来"维持""维生"的生命形式，是无机物的生命形式，比如：岩石、晶体、天体。

简单地说无机的生命让我们感觉到"不会动"。而有机的生命往往让我们感觉到"会动"，而且会"循环地有周期性地动"。也就是说，生命现象，其实是一种链式反应。而且是一种沿着时间的坐标轴，延续很长的链式反应。在这个链式反应的过程中，生命需要不断地与外界交换能量，储蓄的能量比消耗的能量稍微多一点，才能维持在环境中足以克服阻力的运动。

生命中能量的吸收和消耗达到平衡的时候，也就是中医说的："生之本 本于阴阳"，当阴阳平衡的时候，生命就会健康地持续和发展。

与江山共存、与日月同辉的永垂不朽的生命，究竟是"永生"了还是"永死"了？哈哈哈！那就是无机的<原子｜量子>的生命。

5 GRAND UNIFIED THEORY
（大统一理论）

As professor Stephen W Hawking said, when Grand Unified Theory comes into being, it should be a theory that philosophers, scientists and ordinary people can all understand easily and join in the discussion about it. The force that unify all forces is the fictitious force, and therefore all forms of energy ultimately comes from potential energy – that is the grand unified theory.

Fictitious force, or commonly known as "inertial force" comes out of reference, comparison, and relativity.

Reference Frameset

Self wanting to be self

Conatus	Que sera sera	求生存
Nature	今日方知我是我	自然

    Fictitious force is also known as inertial force. Inertial force is all about "self wanting to be self", "self-preservation" or "survival" as in first Newtonian Law: "objects at rest tend to stay at rest, objects in motion tend to stay in motion". Also, when looking at the First Law of thermal dynamics, we will find the same thing: "in a confined system, energy cannot be generated or lost". This is a typical case of "it is what it is".

    Also because fictitious force is not real, therefore a form of "imaginary force". By reasoning, when unifying with artists, one can say all forces are ultimately the force of imagination.

Gravity & electromagnetic force

- **Macro level**
  - Gravity (space wanting to be itself & matter wanting to be itself)

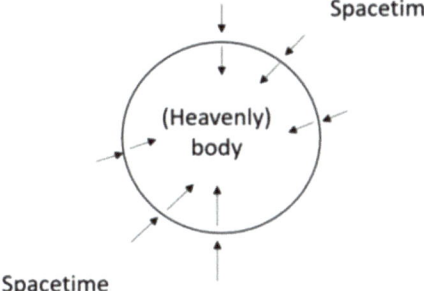

- **Macro level**
  - Electromagnetic force

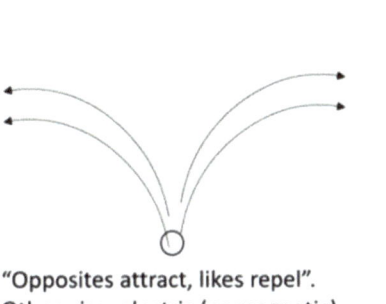

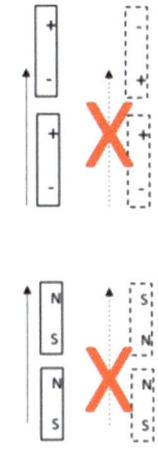

"Opposites attract, likes repel". Otherwise, electric (or magnetic) fields will no longer be itself (or maintaining its identical direction)

Above diagram shows gravity and electromagnetic force are the two states of the same inertial force, when looking from the two different viewpoints of the dual vector space of < in | out >, between space & mass, at a macro level.

Weak force and strong force

- **Micro level**
  - Weak force: Looking within nucleus, particles "self wanting to be itself"

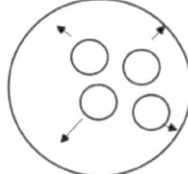

- **Micro level**
  - Strong force: Looking from outside, nucleus "self wanting to be itself" and maintaining its identity

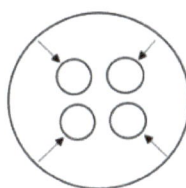

Above diagram shows strong force and week force are the two states of the same inertial force, when looking from the two different viewpoints of the dual vector space of < in | out >, between space & mass, at a micro level.

霍金（Stephen W Hawking）说过，大统一理论一旦被揭示给世人，应该是一个科学家、哲学家、普通人都觉得简单易懂，能够加入讨论的理论。我们每一个人和每一件事，都自己是自己，时时刻刻都趋向于自己做自己。简而言之，这就是大统一理论思想。

无论在社会科学还是在自然科学领域，我们经常可以观察到"自己是自己""自保""维持生存"的现象。从"热力学第一定律"到"牛顿第一定律"都是在描述事物的一种希望延续已经存在的状态的"惯性"。惯性力、自然力、顺势而行的导致"势能"的"（趋）势力"，就是宇宙中 大统一理论所涉及的那种神秘的力量。

以上是宏观宇宙的惯性力。惯性力又叫"想象的力"(fictitious force)。被物理学工作者们认为是一种不实际存在，由于坐标系、参照系的变换产生的力。与艺术工作者们搞大统一思想，可以说：惯性力又是想象力。

以上是微观世界中的惯性力。惯性力又可以称为惰性（inertial force)力。是在没有发生主观能动性的运动的情况下，坐标系与坐标系之间，参照、比对所产生的力。在这些情况下这种"自己要坚持是自己的力"，若与社会科学工作者们搞大统一理论的话，可以统一思想地说：惰性力，是人们好逸恶劳。穷则思变，富则思安；生于忧患，死于安乐……推动着社会进步的力量。

在一个集体，"群"的内部人们窝里斗或是互相关心的力是弱相互作用力。在群体的外部这个坐标系上观察，"物以类聚人以群分"的凝聚力是一种强相互作用力。强相互作用力与弱相互作用力之间是相生相克的。这一双对偶的力就构成了微观世界中的基本粒子核内的强相互作用力和弱相互作用力。

有趣的是，在宏观世界中看，从物体内部到外界的空间之间，跨过交界处，也有着互相之间排斥对抗，以至于物质会弯曲周围的时空的作用力。这种"自己坚持要做自己"的力，就是广义相对论中所提出的想象中的重力。

从物体的内部到外界的时空，跨过交界之处，延长的电场，能使电子排列成同样的"+"和"-"的顺序，使这个形成的方向"自己坚持做自己"的"同性相斥、异性相吸"的力，就是电磁力。

$mc^2 = E = h\nu$

是一个关于有无相生的公式。前一半是相对论的总结。后一半是量子理论的开始。

从一个角度，在一个坐标系中看，观察者能看到宇宙中的物质"从有到无"的能量转换和释放过程。

在另一个对偶的矩阵向量时空中，从另一个角度，在另一个坐标系中看，观察者能看到宇宙中"从无到有"的能量转换和吸收过程。

而原子能和量子能，与所有其他的能量形式一样，最终都是一种势能。能量的来源应该与用哪一种燃料，和在哪个地方开采无关。

6 PERPETUAL-PHOBIA
（永动机恐惧症）

According to the First Law of Thermodynamics, perpetual machine cannot be built in a confined system.
According to the Second Law of Thermodynamics, refrigerator cannot be built in a confined system.
Now that humanity has entered the 21st century, most people have witnessed many refrigerators being built in open systems. When a refrigerator works, provided energy can be absorbed from the outside, heat can continue to dissipate from low temperature regions to higher temperature areas. Such a feat was thought impossible in ancient history for thousands of years.

Next, if we can imagine an open system, the First Law of Thermodynamics can actually guide us on how to build perpetual machine, just like how the Second Law of Thermodynamics once guided humanity on the subject of how to build refrigerators. That is: our imagination really needs to take a quantum jump from "confined systems" to an "open systems".

从"封闭"到"开放"这一"维"来思维的话，世上大致有两种人。

有的人想得开，有的人想不开。

有的人看得开，有的人看不开。

热力学第一定律说，在封闭的体系中能量守恒，能量不可能凭空产生或消失。这使得千百年来，许多人相信永动机是不可能被造出来的。实际上也有许多人把，"永动机是不可能被造出来的"，做为是热力学第一定律的通俗表达方式。

热力学第二定律说，在封闭体系中热不可能从温度低的地方向温度高的地方传播。这使得千百年来人们相信电冰箱是不可能被造出来的。实际上也有许多人曾经把，"电冰箱是不可能被造出来的"，做为是热力学第二定律的通俗表达方式。

但是一转眼人类进入了21世纪。越来越多的人更加想得开，越来越多的人也更加看得开。在开放体系中，电冰箱是可以被造出来的。而且现在普通老百姓家也都可以用上电冰箱了。

在开放体系中永动机其实也随处可见，只是不知道为什么普通的老百姓一直被某些学者们忽悠了。其实我们大家身边的生命现象，就是永动机。电冰箱在开放体系中，吸收能量就可以制冷。动物和植物只要从周围的环境中吸收能量，就可以不断地"动"下去。

Cogito ergo sum.

认识到了就存在了。若把宇宙看做一个封闭体系的化，那么大规模，绝对的永动机是不可能存在的。但是相对的永动机却到处都是。树木、植物其实都是永动机，只不过这些永动机动得比较慢。

动物自然会比植物动得快一点。这样的永动机比较直观，容易观察和理解，究竟是什么装置与外界不断地交换着能量，给永动机提供着最重要的"动机"呢？

绝大多数动物都有着心，而且心连着肺。心和肺从生命的开始到结束，一直周而复始地进行着链式反应的运动，时刻也不能停息。

到此，我们不必再为"制造永动机"这样的科研课题而感到恐惧了吧。"机器人"那么复杂的装置，都已经被许多人制造出来了，制造一两套"机器的心肺系统"，又算得了什么呢？

7 301 CONJECTURE
(301 猜想：呼风唤雨的技术含量)

301 conjecture was made in late 1980's in a dormitory, Room 301 of Building 115, in University of Science & Technology of China. It was inspired by "Goldbach's conjecture", which was very famous in China at the time, although not all students who made 301 conjecture back then fully understood what Goldbach was hypothesizing.

Because Albert Einstein in 1905 publicized a pair of famous equations about properties of light and energy as:

$mc^2 = E = h\nu$

Students living in Room 301, and their frequent visitors, jokingly stated that: there should be practically unlimited amount of energy surrounding everybody, everywhere, every minute, and the reasons were:

1) $E = mc^2$ means everyone's body mass, if multiplied by square of the light speed, would produce the amount of energy, equivalent to tens of thousands of Hiroshima atomic bombs.

2) $E = h\nu$ means every black-body on earth can emit energy through radiation constantly, let alone any other types of "body" or objects with brighter colors.

After 30+ years of work and study, the pursuit of proving "301 conjecture" was unexpectedly yet fatefully connected with proof of "Goldbach's conjecture". Guess after all, every human being on Earth would once in a while, dream of:

Getting something out of nothing, which is:

"Science of dividing by 0", which can only happen when the reference frame is shifted.

After quantum jump from one reference frame to another, anybody can get:
- Real force out of fictitious force
- Utility energy out of potential energy
- Atomic energy out of quantized energy
- Organic life out of inorganic life

"301猜想"是20世纪80年代后期在中国科技大学的115楼301寝室，入住成员和经常来串门的来访者、好朋友们提出来的. 提出这个猜想的原因是因为在那个"学好数理化 走遍天下都不怕"时代哥德巴赫猜想在中国很有名。小伙伴们觉得搞个什么猜想，会显得很有水平，挺有意思的。于是就有人提出了301猜想。但是许多提出301猜想的人们，其实都没有仔细研究过哥德巴赫猜想到底说的是啥。

301猜想的具体内容是：因为阿尔伯特·爱因斯坦在1905年提出了他的，关于光和能量的重要性质的两个公式：

$$mc^2 = E = h\nu$$

在301俱乐部坐着的成员们觉得，每个人，在每个地方，每时每刻，都应该感到身边充满无限的可利用的能量才对。原因是：

1) $E = mc^2$ 表达的意思是，每个人的体重换算成质量，乘以光速的平方，得到的结果应该是几万到十几万个广岛原子弹相当的TNT当量才对；

2) $E = h\nu$ 黑体辐射公式 – 表达的意思是，每种、每个物体，即使是黑色的，也在向外界辐射能量。颜色鲜艳的物体就更会发射出更多的能量了。

经过30多年以后的各种生活和阅历，证明301猜想的推导过程，竟然又出人意料，却又命中注定地与哥德巴赫猜想的证明过程联系在了一起。 我们猜想可能每个人，在漫长的生命过程中，总会有那么某时、某刻、在某地、某环境条件下，梦想着这世上要是能"不劳而获"、"一劳永逸"、能够少干活多拿钱，能从"无中生有"，忽悠别人说："见证奇迹的时刻到了"，该有多好？

"无中生有"的学问也就是"除以0的科学"，只能发生在参照系和坐标系变换了以后，技术含量其实不是很高。任何人一学就会，每家每户都可很快投入使用，迅速创收、获利。

在发生了量子的能级跳跃和参照系、坐标系变换以后，就很容易达到以下"无中生有"的效果：

- 从虚力(惯性力)产生实力

- 从潜能(势能)产生家用、工业用能源

- 从量子能产生原子能

- 从无机的生命进化到有机的生命

8 SCIENCE OF DIVIDING BY 0 – study of dimensions
(除以 0 的科学 – 思维学)

Among researchers who study number theories, "dividing by 0", "infinity" and "infinitesimal" are the taboo topics, because historically, students of "number theories" had the natural tendency to refuse treating "number theory" as part of the "group theory". Numbers in number theories often reflect projections of numbers from multi-dimensional groups interacting in universes which possesses far more dimensions than 1 or 2. When a number is divided by 0, much like how -1 was taken a square-root by mathematicians hundreds of years ago, numbers in one dimension are logically and rigorously associated with numbers in another dimension. Only after realizing this from the perspective of multi-dimensional space-time, can we appreciate the improvements and significance of "dividing by 0", as being of such great contributions to the further perfection of the number theories.

The following equations form a list of important ingredients and necessities, sorely missed in today's number theories.

$x / 0 = y$ (electromagnetic or other forms of "inductions": for instance, electrical current induce magnetic fields in a shifted reference frame-set)

$0 / 0 = h$ (because $h*0=0$; uncertainty principle; history "h" always has a certain percentage of lies)

$1 / 0 = 0.5h, -0.5h$ (setting the unit for the "history number" as "h", and set quantum gap for natural number to be 0.5h, like 1/2 spin in quantum theory)

$-1 / 0 = -0.5h, 0.5h$ (same as above)

$A \equiv A$ (a number is identical to itself in the same dimension)

$A \not\equiv B$ (two numbers cannot be identical when dimensions or reference frames are different)

With the above equations, the number theory has just become much more mature and more reflective of the multidimensional nature of our universe. With "infinity" and "infinitesimal" better depicted and within our scope of study, many of the conjectures of the past centuries, such as: Riemann Hypothesis, Goldbach's conjecture, twin prime conjecture…can be easily proven.

Now let's look at how x / 0 = y is deducted:

数论研究者中好像有一种有意避开谈"除以 0"和"无穷大/小"的倾向，因为以往的数论研究者们没有把数论做为包含在群论和抽象代数中的一门学问来对待。数论中研究的数，只能反应多维的数字空间在一维中、一条坐标轴中的投影。当一个数除以 0 的时候，正像多年前有人提出-1 的平方根等于 i 以后，一维中的数与另一维中的数就被联系起来了。只有这样，数论的研究发展才能达到更完善。

而下面的公式也正好展示了到今天为止，数论研究中所缺乏和需要的。

x / 0 = y （坐标系之间的"感应"：电磁；风雨）

0 / 0 = h （因为 0=h*0，测不准原理，历史和将来一样，总有一定成份的虚假、不确定性）

1 / 0 = 0.5h, -0.5h （确立"悟空数"的单位"h"，以及自然数的最小量子化间隔为 0.5h）

-1 / 0 = -0.5h, 0.5h （与上同）

$A \equiv A$ （同一维中，自己恒等于自己）

$A \not\equiv B$ （不同一维中，有条件的相等不是恒等）

应该说：有了以上公式以后，数论做为一个数学理论才变得更加成熟和更能反应宇宙的现实。不惧怕谈"无限大"、"无限小"之后，一些数论的猜想，如：黎曼猜想，哥德巴赫猜想，孪生质数猜想……也就可以得到轻易的证实。

下面看一看 x / 0 = y 是怎么推导出来的？

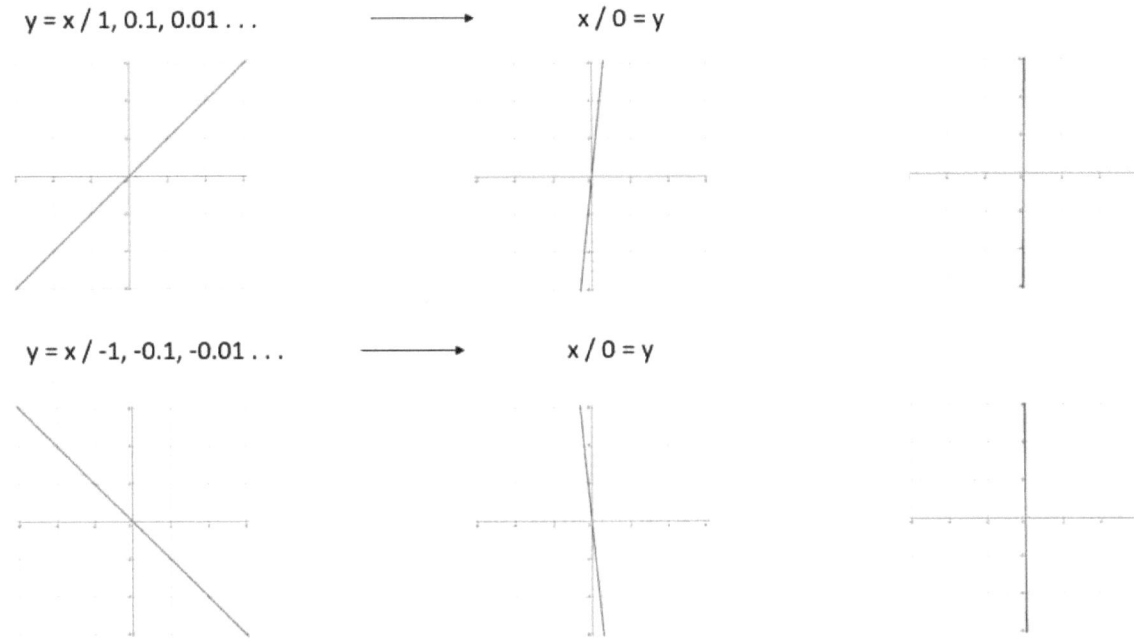

Now let's look at how the unit of "history number" is established. Because this dimension "y" is merged from two opposite directions, the unit "1h" is split by the real value "0" in the middle.

现在让我们来看看思维、进化 的"悟空"数的单位 h （history），是怎样建立的？。因为这新的一维 "y" 是从两个不同的方向，演化合并而来的。那么这个新的单位 "1h" 也就被数字 "0" 给从中对半分开了。

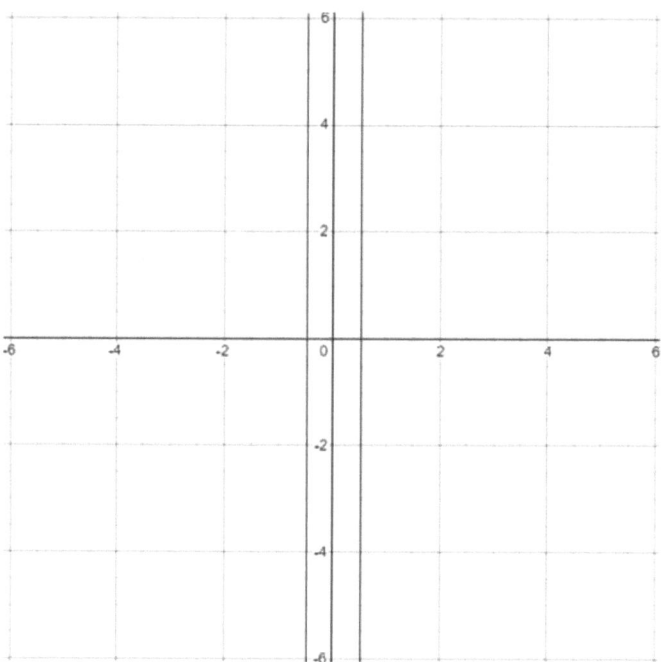

The establishment and evolution of the above unit "h" for "history number" is the proof of Riemann hypothesis. Because the original Riemann hypothesis was observed between the 2 dimensions of "real number" and "complex numbers". Now when we can witness the same relationship between the 2 dimensions of "real number" and "history number", then the inter-dimensional relationship defined in the hypothesis is "confirmed", a.k.a. "proven". An additional reminder to support such claim is: among inter-dimensional observations, there is no difference in status among "reference frame-set" or "dimensions". All dimensions (real number vs. complex number; real number vs. history number) are interchangeable, no matter in the Cartesian xyz coordinate system or Einstein's xyz-t coordinate system, in abstract algebra.

Like in the numbering system of "complex number", there are "real part" and "imaginary part", if we make "history number" to equivalently possess "real part" and "story part", then Goldbach's Conjecture becomes to prove numbers in the groups of "history number", the following equation is true "1+ah = 0.5+bh + 0.5+ch" in "real part". That is to prove "1=0.5+0.5", need I say more? It is as proven as being "self-evident".

Aha, don't forget about the "infinite twin prime conjecture" here either. Since Euclid has already proven there are infinite amount of prime numbers thousands of years ago, and now we have observed in the multiple dimensional space-time, (for prime numbers >3) the minimum prime number gap is "1h" in history number, or a projection of "2" in real number. "1h" or "2" are the dimensions module that can be used to solve modulus to determine prime number among nature numbers. Therefore it is proven, there has to be infinite twin prime numbers among natural numbers, or otherwise we would have been 1) disputing with Euclid; 2) letting second part of natural number changing the dimensions of minimal gap module "1h" or "2" for the first part of the natural numbers. 1) and 2) would both be irrational.

以上推到演化和建立"悟空数"的单位"h"的过程，就是黎曼猜想成立的证据。黎曼猜想是一个跨越两"维"之间（实数&虚数"维"）观察到的现象。我们现在也跨越两"维"之间（实数&悟空数"维"）观察到了同样的现象。根据相对论的原则，坐标系统之间，也就是维与维之间，在抽象代数中是地位均等可以互相替代的。

如同在复数系统中，有"实部"和"虚部"一样，在悟空数系统中，也有"实部"和"空部"。于是证明哥德巴赫猜想的数学问题也就变成了：如何证明在悟空数所组成的"群"中，"1+ah = 0.5+bh + 0.5+ch"在"实部"是相等的。1=0.5+0.5，这还用证明吗？简直是不言自明啊！

对了，不能忘了证明"孪生质数猜想"。几千年前欧几里得已经证明过在自然数中有无穷多个质数。上面我们提到了，在二维的时空中的观察现象是，大于 3 的质数间的最小间隔"1h"，投影在自然数范围内是"2"，这是一个"模"的尺寸、内维数。所以在自然数的集合中也就会有无穷多对孪生质数。不然我们就浪费了欧几里得聪明的反证法和令人信服的证明，或者试图用自然数的后半部改变前半部中定义的"1h"或"2"的最小间隔模量维数。得到的矛盾的结果是不可能成立的。

9 SYMMETRY AND ASYMMETRY
（对称和不对称）

In Greek, the word "symmetry" meant "of measurement" or "about measurement" (sym metry). Therefore, things that can be precisely measured are "symmetrical", and when things cannot be precisely measured, are "asymmetrical".

With the above statement and knowing that we have entered a quantum age, where uncertainty principle rules the world, it is important for us to realize that everything we observe in the universe is symmetrical and asymmetrical at the same time, depending on the view point, from which we observe.

简单地说：对称就是某一种形式的相等。

自对称、镜像对称、旋转对称、成比例对称……

也就是：

自己等于自己，照镜子以后等于自己，旋转了以后等于自己，成比例放大以后等于自己……

简单地说：不对称就是自己不等于自己。

从以上的定义中，我们可以看到：在一个封闭体系中，或者自己非常接近自己本体的时候，"自己不等于自己"，或者说"不对称"，是不可能的。成语"原形毕露"说的就是这个道理。

沿着"人不能第二次踏进同一条河流"的思路分析，当一个物体，从一个时空走进另一个时空的时候，"自己等于自己"，也就是"自对称"，就成了不可能发生的事了。

所以变化无常是常态。永恒的坚持不存在。

或者说：道可道非常道，万事皆空……

这样的话语才是描述宇宙中一切现象的真谛。

既然是这样，我们现在就知道了，宇宙中的对称和不对称总是同时存在的。因为时空是一个永无止境、川流不息的河流。东方文化中把我们在宇宙中居住的最近的部分时空称为"银河"。太阳系围着银河中心的黑洞，大约每 2 亿 5 千万年左右绕一圈。也就是说，我们在太阳系中看着对称的所有的现象，若是被拿到银河系中去观察的时候就会感觉他们都不是那么对称了。

"对称"这个词中，有一个"对"字。这就说明这个概念，至少需要两个成分。成双成对才能谈对称，即使是自对称也得把自己分成两个"一半"，做到至少"一分为二"。所以对称是一个从"数论"演化到 "群论"的数学概念，是一个从"singularity"演化到"duality"的物理概念，是一个从"个体"演化到"集体"的社会概念，是一个从"individuality"演化到"polity"的政治、军事概念……

当人们把自对称、镜像对称、旋转对称、成比例对称……像加减乘除，平方开方一样地进行复合运算以后，得出来的结果，也就是叠加的复合对称，往往就会被人们看成是"不对称"。

由以上的推导我们可以看出，"不对称"来源于"对称"。

因为负负得正：

我们又可以推导出"对称"的起源是"不对称"。如此循环往复、周而复始。

除法，做为一个成比例对称的运算方法，有着一个"比例"的"比"字。当人们比较"投资"与"回报"，"付出"与"收获"，心里面梦想、期盼着"一本万利"，"或者不劳而获"的时候，就要运用到÷0 的科学。按照前一章所描述的计算结果：$x,y,z……÷0= y,z,x ……$一根坐标轴上的数÷0 的结果，得到另一根与之垂直相交、线性无关的坐标轴上去找。

也就是说，想要进行"从无到有"或者"无中生有"的不对称运算的话，在一"维"中的运算，结果得到另一"维"中去寻找。虽然得到的结果是一个测不准的未知数，可是控制得好的话，也可能有一个令人惊喜的效果。

10 VIRTUAL WORK AND REAL WORK
（虚功和有用功）

In 18th century, Jean Le Rond d'Alembert studied extensively about the "imaginary", "fictitious" and "inertial" force and the concept of "virtual work". Since then, not many scientists put too much thoughts on getting useful "work" out of something unreal or imagined.

At the beginning of 20th century, Albert Einstein came up with his theories of lights ($mc^2 = E = h\nu$) by studying the shift of reference framesets. But still, the dots were not connected between atomic energy and "work" that could be done by "imagination", or something that is "virtual", or "0", or being "lazy".

Now entering 21st century and knowing what we know about "quantum", "vacuum" and "ether", it has eventually become conceivable and practical to get substantial force out of stringing together fictitious force; and get real work out of virtual work. The "stringing together" is called "chain reaction".

Voila! Humanity have just discovered inexhaustible amount of stable and flexible renewable energy that can be used to power the evolution of a "future human race" for generations to come.

功的数学公式是：

功 = 力 x 距离

当"力"或者"距离"，两项之中的一项等于 0 的时候，计算出来的"功"的结果就等于 0 了。

虚功是一种"想象"的功。比如：当一个人使出吃奶的劲，去推一块巨大无比的岩石，而岩石纹丝不动的时候。岩石移动的距离为 0。人的手伸展出去的距离也为 0，但是做着"推"的动作的人，有可能已经满头大汗，耗费了许多的能量了，想象着做了许多的功，但是做的都是"虚功"。

另外有一种"虚功"是：移动的距离很大，但是发现没有任何的发力者在周围施力、使劲。比如在地球表面的河流，除了运河以外，很难见到流得长的河流会有笔直的河道。而且运河中的水流的时间长了以后，河道也会开始变得弯弯曲曲。扭曲河道的这些大自然鬼斧神工的侵蚀力，没有任何的发力者。把河流扭得弯弯曲曲的力，是一种惯性力，想象力，是坐标系变换所产生的力。

以惯性力×很长的距离，计算结果得出来的"功"也是"虚功"。

通过以上的描述，我们可以看到，如果想要从"虚功"之中提取"有用功"的话：

1）需要有坐标系的变换；

2）需要定位、找到哪一个坐标系内有着能为人利用的"有用功".

用"惯性力""懒惰的力量""潜力"这些"虚力"，来做"借力打力"这样"不劳而获""一本万利""四两拨千斤"的大事业，需要找对"发力点"所在的坐标系，还需要认准"借力处"所在的另一个坐标系。

这样才能以正确的方式获取能量，发展生产力，推动社会进步。

在前面讨论过"÷0 的科学"以后，我们就会发觉：其实想要从"虚功"之中产生"有用功"，也是一个"无中生有""从小到大""从无到有""好逸恶劳"的物理问题。同时，这也是一个分母为 0 的除法的数学问题。

11 A NEW INDUSTRY
（一个新的行业）

To get "something out of nothing" or to get "hard power out of soft power", and get energy out of thin air, etc.... have all become possible with the rise of an industry that can explore and apply Grand Unified Energy (a.k.a. Universal Energy) for domestic use in average households. Grand Unified Energy consists of quantum energy and atomic energy. According to First Law of thermodynamics, energy cannot be generated in the universe, but can only be converted from one form to another. At a microlevel, when utilizing atomic energy or quantum energy, smaller the particle sizes are, higher the efficiency is for the energy conversion process.

从原子能到量子能，从物质世界到数字、量子的世界，从原子时代进入量子时代，一两项发明是不足以推动一个行业的。所以下面我们会不断推出量子化能源在工农生产、交通运输、日常生活各领域更多的应用产品。一旦量子化大气动力、呼吸为机理的能源利用被深刻理解之后，大家会发现气动能源与电动能源一样有效、便利，有时在某些方面甚至会有特殊的优点，技高一筹。

量子能开矿设备制造

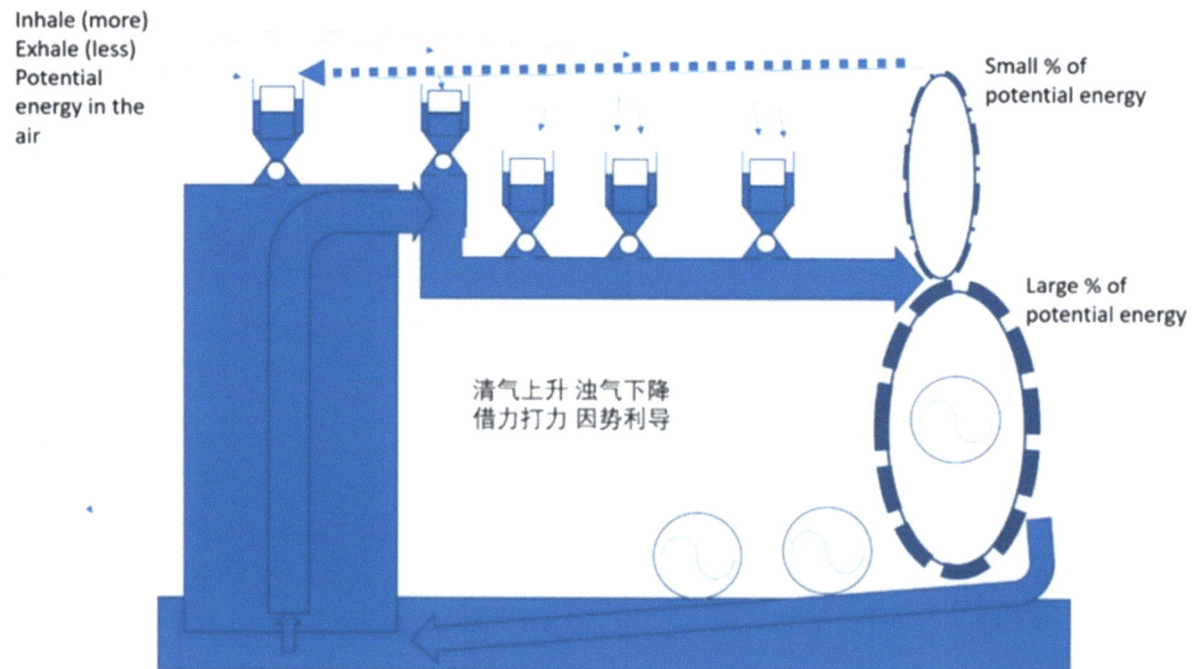

量子能发应堆

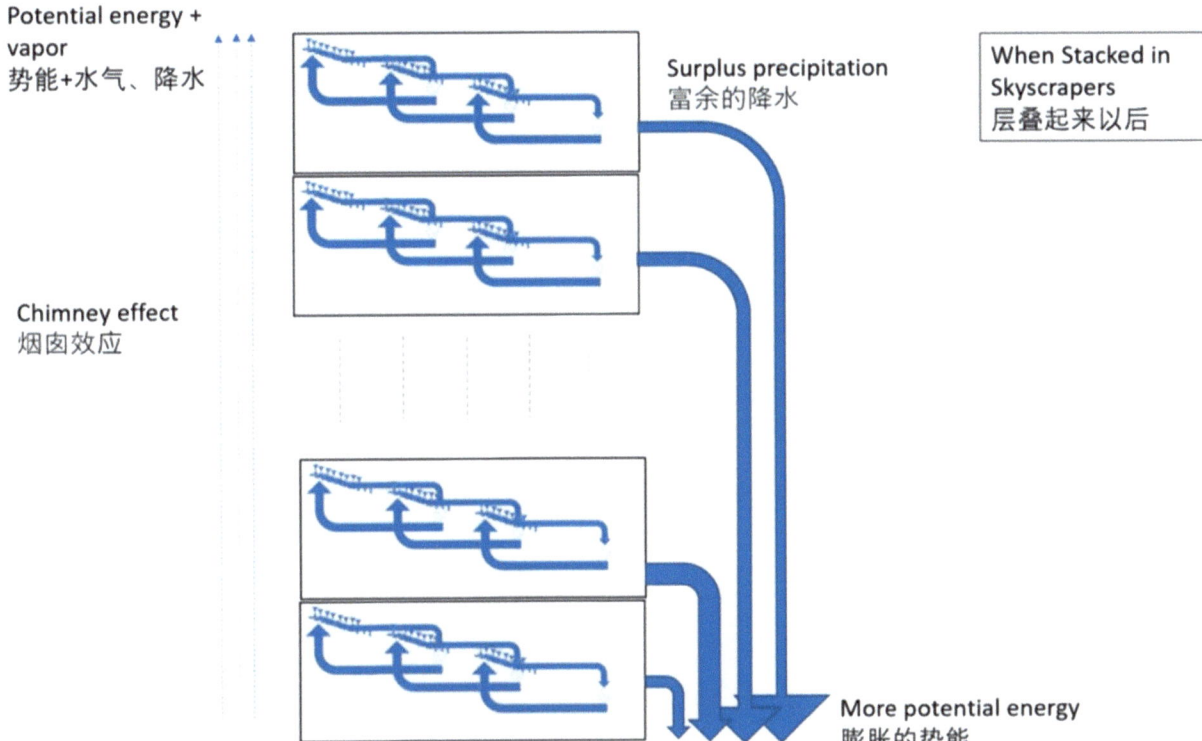

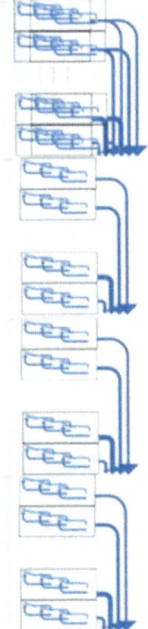

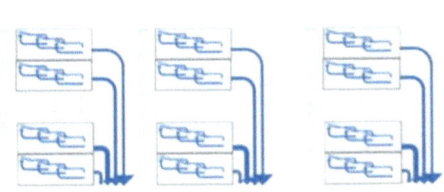

Small buildings to become green buildings
(self-sufficient for clean water and energy)
小楼房可成为绿色建筑物
清洁用水、清洁能源自给自足）

Skyscrapers can become quantum energy reactors
(supply surrounding communities with clean water and energy)
大高楼可形成量子能反应堆
为周边社区提供清洁用水、清洁能源）

量子能航行器

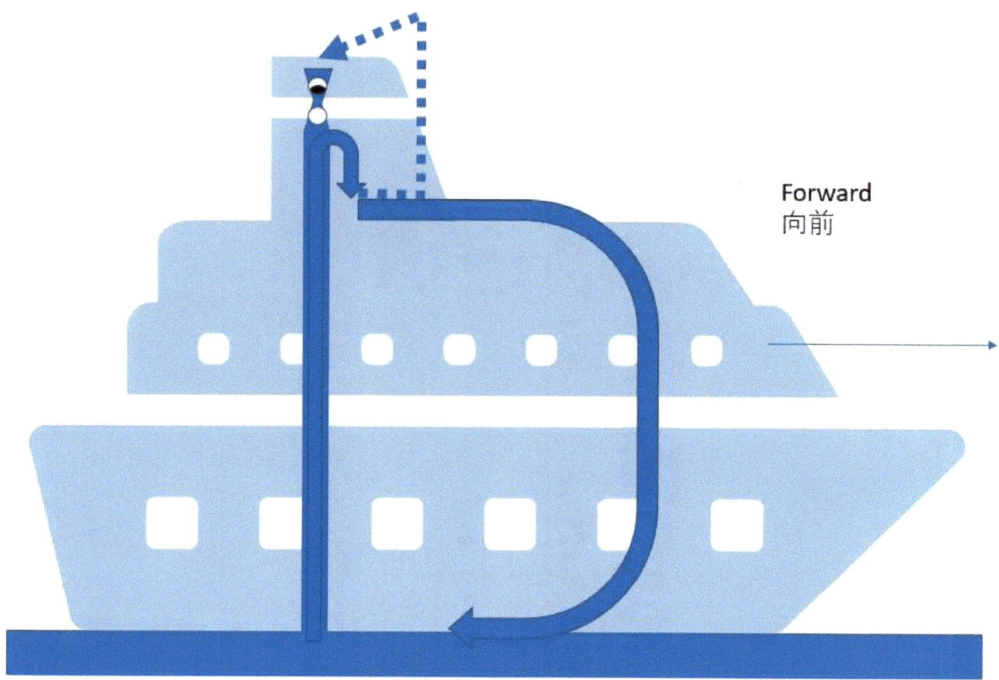

Forward
向前

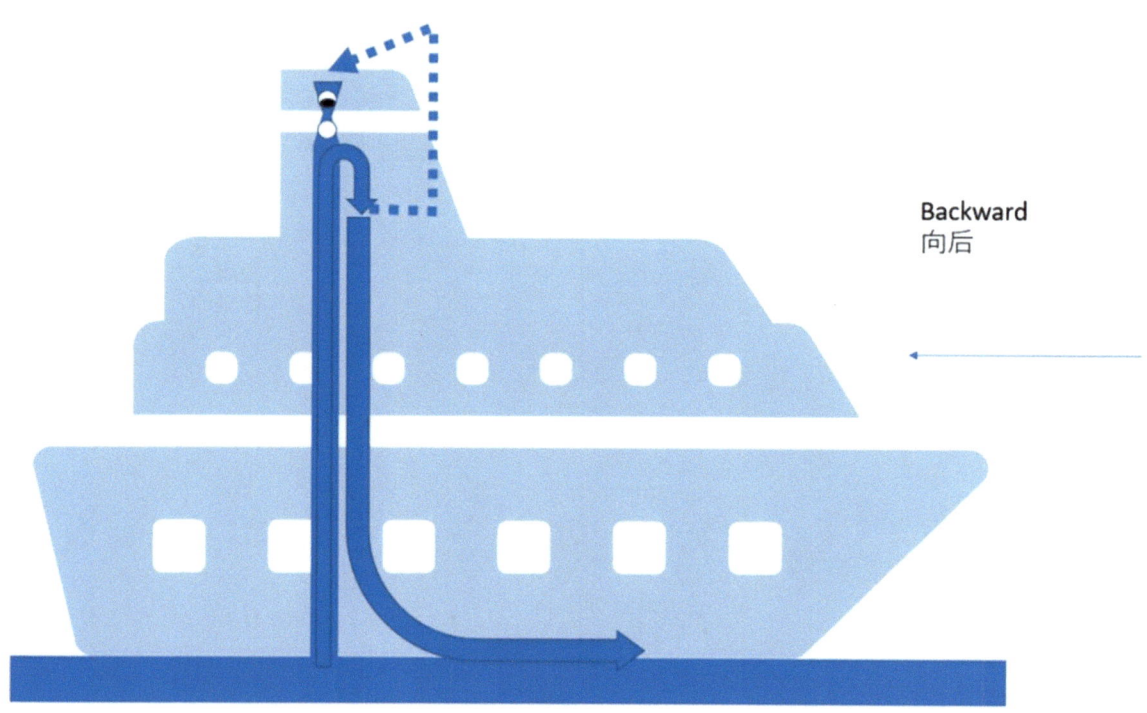

Backward
向后

量子能航行器

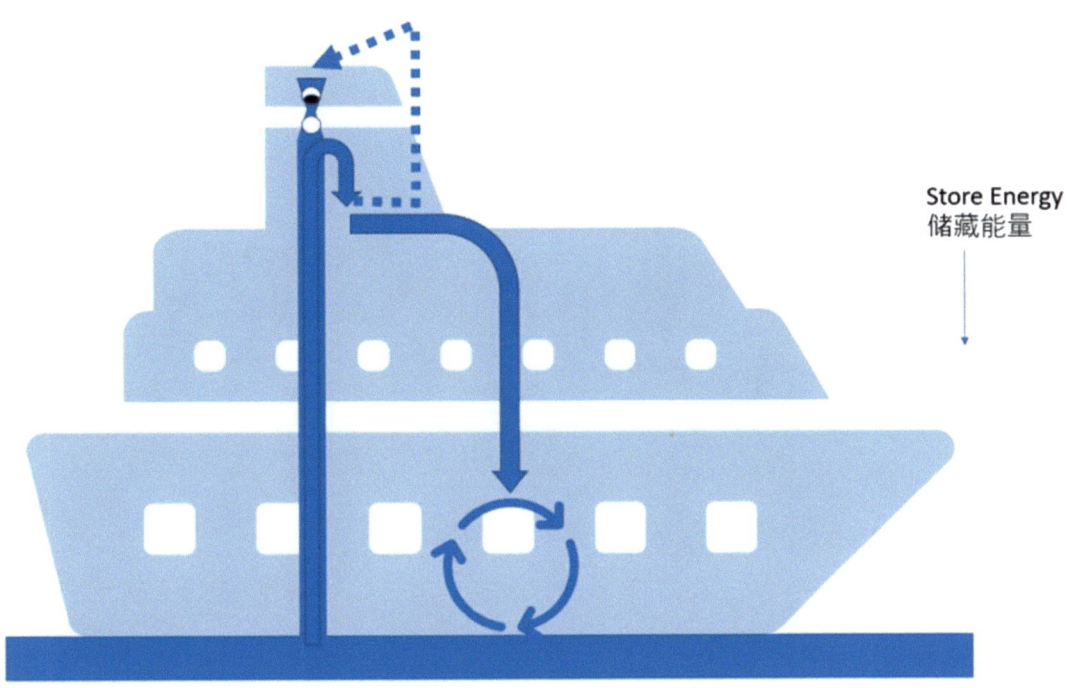

Store Energy
储藏能量

量子能飞行器

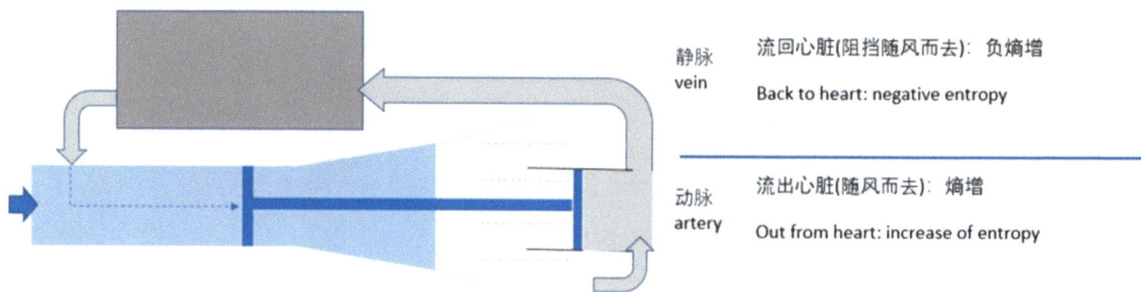

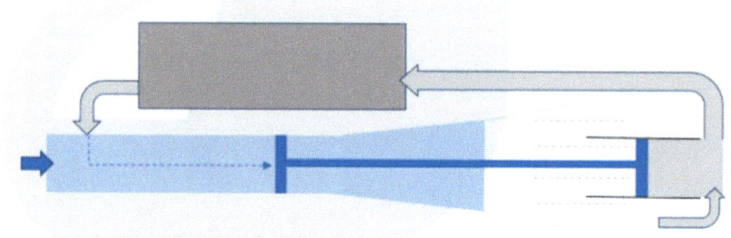

居民发电站

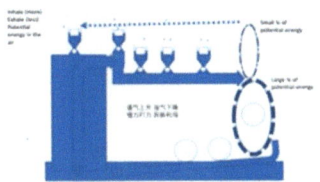

健身房发电站

量子能水耕栽培

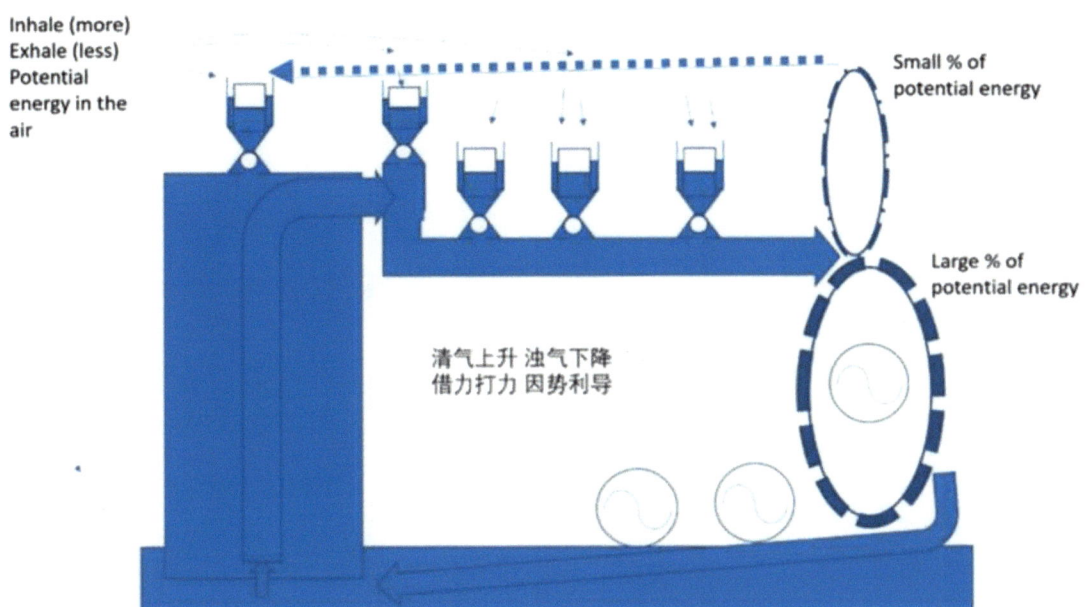

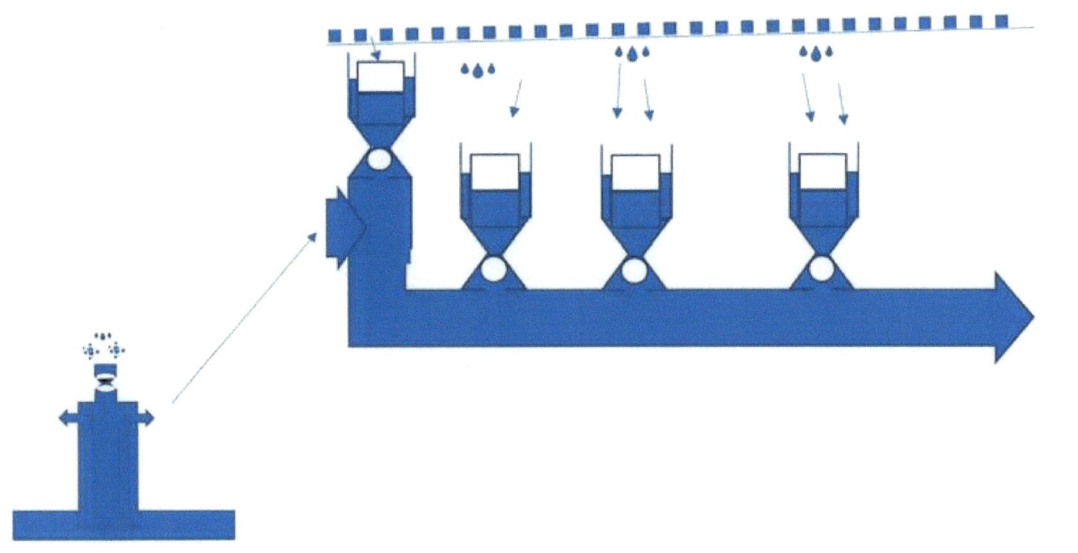

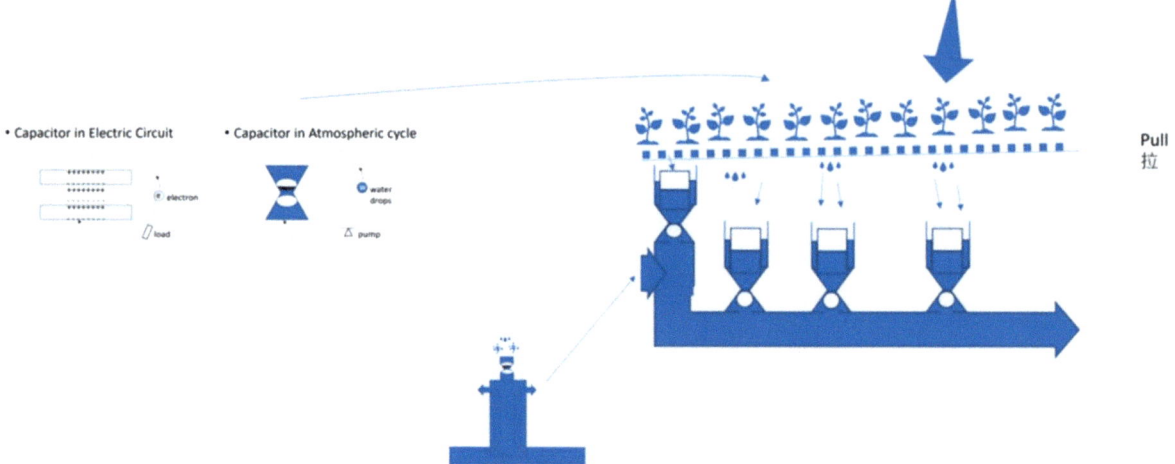

12 RELIGION, SCIENCE & IMAGINATION
(宗教观)

It is hard to imagine "God", "Magic", "Science", "iMagination", or even "Language", these "many" things are "one and the same", but they are. Just like the imagination of an elephant is the summary imagination of all the parts. The belief system of the future would simply be the evolved sum of all the belief systems existing in the universe today.

Professor Stephen W Hawking stated in his famous book "a brief history of time", "the ultimate triumph of human reason" that philosophers, scientists and ordinary people can all participate in discussing, is to know "the mind of God".

Einstein's famous quote about believing Spinoza's God is often cited as evidence by religious people, as proof that religion is not a contradiction of modern science.

With advancement of science and its strength in quantitative analysis today, one significant progress made in the 21st century that can unify all belief systems is that: God is omnipresent, omnipotent and omniscient. God has a body mass = 0 kg to every observer and with the density the same as that of the background radiation of the universe. Such body mass is undetectable just like "ether", it varies slightly in different regions of the universe, but always close to vacuum, 0, "empty" or "no existent".

古代人对许多自然现象无法解释的时候，心里面就产生了神。有的古代人还用口述的方法世代相传地传下来一些传说。后来有了文字以后，这些传说会被人记录下来，有时会被某些人与历史混在一起，然后在这些传说的历史的基础上往往就产生了宗教。许多宗教中，都会产生一些"偶像"型人物。

魔术是某些聪明而有能力的人，通过巧妙的设计和技巧展示一些人们无法解释的自然现象。魔术师在西方语言里面叫："magician"，其实要深入研究下去的话，"mag-"的词头跟亚洲的（南越）"大兽"或"象"关系还挺大。

总之，无论是"偶像"还是"魔术"，都跟"想象力"有着紧密的联系。随着人类社会的发展，人们觉得运用科学来解释自然现象似乎更接近真实。而"真实使你得自由"，所以真理对人类来说是不可抗拒的。

万事皆空，无常，无厚入有间

（注释：以上这些说法都是对"全知、全能、全在"的，宇宙背景辐射的不同形式的描述）

道可道非常道

（同上解释）

真理将使你得自由

（注释：真空对周围物质的吸引是不可抗拒的）

全知、全能、全在

（注释：宇宙背景辐射，真空，以太的性质）

无论看哪个方向看，都有着阿拉的面孔

（解释同上）

宇宙背景辐射

(20 世纪人类文明进步的路程碑，现代科学技术的探测结果)

单位质量=0，密度=0

(神、以太、第五元素、黑物质、悟空、如来佛、宇宙背景辐射、宙斯、雷、电、电磁场、光……的性质)

13 TRUE AND FALSE
（真假观）

In normal Boolean operation, "true and false = false" and as discussed earlier when talking about symmetry, "true" cannot exist without "false", therefore true and false always exist together in the universes, in every spacetime.

From the above statements, we can deduct everywhere in the universe, there is unified true and false, and we normally observe falsehood everywhere. As King Solomon said it best: vanity of vanities; all is vanity.

Taking an abstractive view of history, Nicolaus Copernicus, Galileo Galilei, Isaac Newton, Albert Einstein, all made their famous discoveries beginning with studying objects in a moving transportation vehicle. When an object is observed as "at rest" inside the vehicle, it is false to say it is "at rest" outside of the vehicle. Since the Solar system is like a large vehicle moving in the Milky Way, the dualistic quantum state of <true | false> also apply when describing everything on Earth, in Solar system, Milky Way, or any larger regions of universe, as being "at rest" and "in motion" at the same time.

Every real number is, in other perspectives, attached with an imaginary number, a history number, and many, many more numbers from other dimensions...

$a = a + 0i + 0h + 0...$

One's body cannot exist without its environment.

没有环境就没有本体

真情报、假情报汇总在一起才是完全的情报

真新闻、假新闻都听了才算听完了所有的新闻

真实的现实、假想的现实加在一块儿形成的是更真实的扩增现实

总而言之，言而总之，即使我们生活的宇宙中充满了虚假和不真实，我们也是可以生活得非常滋润，非常幸福的。我们可以豪迈地说："让暴风雨来得更猛烈些吧"。

然后从虚假中提取精神食粮，从真空中获得温饱，喝西北风也能转化成高营养的卡路里。从想象力中获得生命力。

可以说原子和量子，就是那么一个"真假"的存在的关系。而他们的存在，又是互相之间离不开的。< 原子是"真实"存在的物质（$mc^2=E$）| 量子是虚假存在的宇宙背景辐射（$E=hv$）>。核强相互作用力的产生是因为：原子若没有外界的宇宙背景辐射把它压在一起的话，就散开了，不存在了。核弱相互作用力的产生是因为：量子的宇宙背景辐射若没有原子对他施加的抵抗力的话，也就延

伸、压入原子，变形了。

真的和假的总是同时存在的一个统一体，这种现象也是对"测不准原理"或者叫"不确定性原理"的一种抽象的想象。

真和假离不开，生命和周围的环境、坐标系、参照系离不开。生命过程只是一个与周围环境进行物质和能量交换的过程。而我们周边生活的宇宙环境，是一个非常复杂的环境，是有许多、许多的宇宙，而且每个宇宙是有着许多、许多的"维"，互相影响着、感应着。

14 UNITY AND FUTURE
（全球观、将来观）

Immanuel Kant proposed that time and space are of mere imagination out of human psyche. Such a theory has been scientifically proven again and again ever since, especially after theory of relativity. Recently published scientific paper and research works further theorized such imagination in popular books like "a brief history of time".

Kant also predicted global democracy would bring eternal peace to the world, which subject to how each blind person interpret and imagine his or her elephant, is mostly true. Based on the future view of the Grand Unified Theory, war and peace is of one unity, more or less like how General Ferdinand Foch said to have commented after Treaty of Versailles: "This isn't peace, it's a truce of 20 years". Therefore, if we take a particle-wave duality view of the history interspersed by war and peace, World War I is a ½ spin particle, the 20 year armistice in between is a superposition of many full spin particles piled together. Then there is another ½ spin of war particle as World War II, followed by many superpositions of full spin particles into a "peace" known as "cold war". Such cycle continues in spacetime and will continue farther into the future, as eternal as Kant predicted.

If "war and peace" can be unified in a Grand Unified Theory and can be written in a mixture of languages and cultures (just like the famous novel "War and Peace" was), then uniting other substances or concepts in natural or social science could all turn into a proverbial "piece of cake".

At the beginning of 20th century, Albert Einstein came up with his theories of lights ($mc^2 = E = h\nu$) by studying the shift of reference framesets. But still, the connections were not made between atomic energy and "work" that could be done by "imagination", or something that is "virtual", or "0", or being "lazy".

Now entering 21st century and knowing what we know about "quantum", "vacuum" and "ether", it has eventually become conceivable and practical to get substantial force out of stringing fictitious force together; and get real work out of virtual work.

Now that unification is achieved, Humanity have just discovered inexhaustible amount of stable and flexible renewable energy that can be used to identify the roads to the evolution of the future human race.

世界语：世界所有语言加起来、融合后的集合

世界民族：世界所有民族加起来、融合后的集合

大统一理论其实质，归根到底是一个将物质世界和精神世界统一为一体的理论。当然，任何理论都不可能与古代同名的理论，比如："阴阳统一"，"天人合一"的理论，保持形式和实质上的等同。人不能第二次踏进同一条河流，因为人已经不是那个人，而河流也已经不是那一条河流。

如果说到在21世纪量子时代以后的大统一理论相对于以前的大统一理论有什么不同的话，那就是这种统一以后的"一体"对内是可分的，同时对外又是离不开群体和大环境的。

在20世纪以前，人类没有家用电冰箱，也没有在天上到处穿行的飞机，没有随处可见的无线电

通讯……

在 21 世纪以前，人类因特网没有普及，手机也不常见……

许多以前觉得不太可能的事情，在人类社会的发展过程中，忽然一个时空过去了，就全都变成现实了。

呼风唤雨曾经被认为是现实生活中不可能的事情。可是在 21 世纪后，突然进步到了另一个时空，大家发觉风雨呼唤器在每家每户都可能出现，而且甚至还有可能在每个写字台上出现。

在人类从古以来的众多梦想中，既然飞天能够成为现实，隐身，其实也不是一件很难做到的事情。所有的物体都是阴和阳两个方面的统一体。

若要隐藏物体的阴影，只需要根据制造手术台上无影灯的口诀，来设计周围的背景灯光安排，就大功告成了。那个口诀就是：一个灯，一个影；多个灯，多个影；灯越多，影越淡；群灯群影，无影灯……

上面说了如何隐藏物体的阴影，若是要隐藏物体的阳面，只要像变色龙一样，按下面的设计给物体穿上一件外衣就可以了。

一面屏，一个景；多个屏，多个景；屏越多，景越隐；大隐结庐在人境……

One set
一套摄像头和显示屏

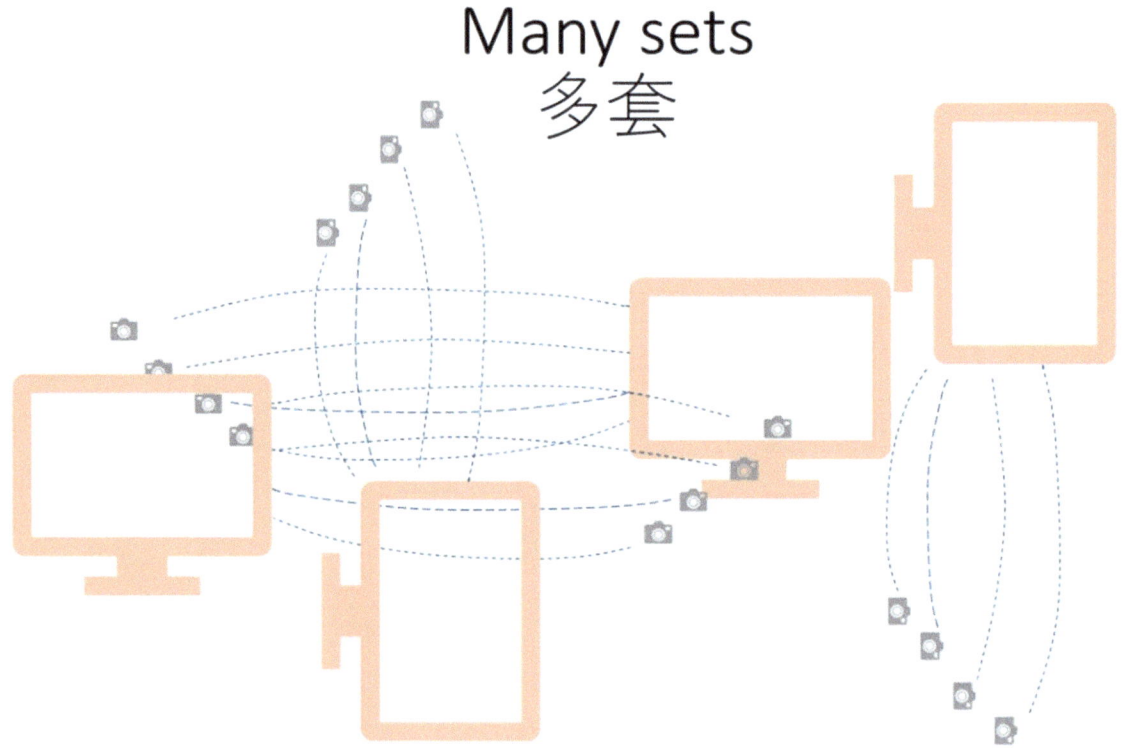

Many sets
多套

Many sets woven around a polyhedron
围绕着多面体编制起来

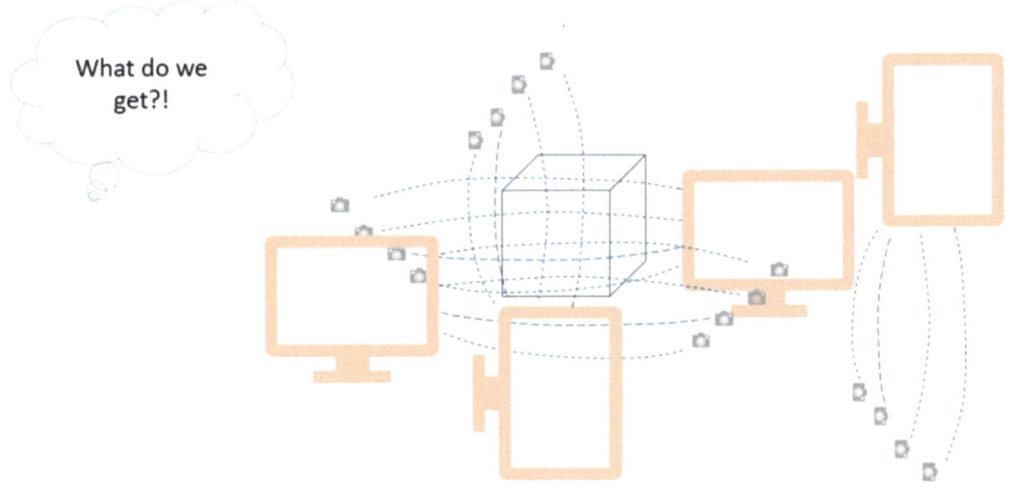

想要面面俱到的表演者，最终将消失于无形。

在<原子|量子>物质、能量、理论、行动，大统一的世界里，也就是阴阳平衡的现实宇宙中，正所谓大方无隅，大音稀声，大器晚成、大象无形……大巧若拙，大勇若怯，大智若愚……

后大统一理论的时空中，任何"一"个答案都不只是一个简单的数论的答案，而是一个复杂的群论研究结果的表格式的、矩阵式的、有条件的、有前提、有上下文的答案，是"辩证的、一分为二"的答案，是"具体问题，具体情况，具体分析"的答案。比如若有人问到：将来的人们将以什么样的形式分配社会财富的时候，应该说"按资分配"，"按劳分配"，"按需分配"都不是一个正确的答案。但是把所有的答案放在一起，描绘出来的景象，就能让许多人满意了，那就是：

老幼病残者 – 按需分配

年富力强者 – 按劳、按资，加权平均优化分配

根据爱因斯坦的质能公式，或者普朗克的量能公式，每个人都有着几万到十几万颗广岛原子弹

的能量储备。若每个人充分发挥所持有的能量的话，想发动战争损害他人的话，参战者都将是最终的失败者，会不可避免地因此成为达尔文奖获得者。

而和平、自由、公平地通过正常的阴阳平衡的新陈代谢方式与外界交换卡路里的生命，将获得永生。

当有人问到圣雄甘地，他如何能够对非暴力一定能够战胜当时不可一视的大英帝国充满信心的时候，甘地回答说：当某人对某人施暴的时候，他好像在全人类的心理上，种下了一点量子意义上的仇恨的种子。当某个人做正义的事情的时候，不知道从什么地方，就会无中生有地冒出无数神秘的人物来帮助他　(When someone commits violence, he does something to the human psyche of the entire humanity. When someone works on something that is righteous and just, he will get help from people springing up, out of nowhere or from everywhere)。

人类与其在同类中以"窝里斗"的形式来掠夺财富谋生的话，不如从更低一点的生命形式，也就是从永动机中获得财富，更安全有效一些。

后人有诗赞曰：

如意弹，满天星
纵横四海 养人情
xyz 除以 0
不战而屈天下兵
。

ABOUT THE AUTHOR

David Chen is a computer scientist with background in environmental study and Earth and Space Science. He is a firm believer that this book would not have been possible without the help from others, therefore he believe this "about the author" section should include his environment and surrounding, many people and events he had encountered, which would be too numerous to enumerate.

南郭求败，成分主要是一群滥竽充数的电脑码农，曾混迹于环保和地球与空间科学行业。

"南郭"表达的是："混日子"、"不劳而获"、"蹭别人的流量"的远大志向；

"求败"表达的是："一生求一败，而不可得"的高手境界。

所以南郭先生相信这本书的作者与"文章本天成，妙手偶得之"那句话，说的是同一个笔杆子－也就是一个时空，一群有缘人吧。

www.ingramcontent.com/pod-product-compliance
Lightning Source LLC
Chambersburg PA
CBHW041533040426
42446CB00002B/68